A Working Mother's Guide to Blockchain and Cryptocurrency

Maggie Webber

Disclaimer

This book is presented solely for educational and entertainment purposes. The author, publisher and their respective affiliates are not offering it as legal, investment, or other professional services advice. All investment/financial opinions expressed by the author are from personal research and experience and are intended as informational material. While best efforts have been used in preparing this book, the author and publisher make no representations or warranties of any kind and assume no liabilities with respect to the accuracy or completeness of the contents, and specifically disclaim any implied warranties of merchantability or fitness of use for a particular purpose. Neither the author nor the publisher shall be held liable or responsible to any person or entity with respect to any loss or incidental or consequential damages caused, or alleged to have been caused, directly or indirectly, by the information contained herein. Any use of this information is at your own risk.

You should not treat any opinion expressed in this book as a specific inducement to make a particular investment or follow a particular strategy, but only as an expression of opinion. You should be aware of the real risk of loss in following any strategy or investment discussed in this book. Before acting on the information contained herein, you should assess whether it is suitable for your individual circumstances, and strongly consider seeking advice from your own financial or investment advisor.

Other Books by Maggie

This book is the 8th in a series of "Working Mother's Guides". The others are:

- A Working Mother's Guide to a Guilt-Free Career (An Amazon Best-Seller)
- A Working Mother's Guide to the 4 P's
- A Working Mother's Guide to the Way Up from Down
- A Working Mother's Guide on how to Toss Your Boss
- A Working Mother's Guide on Eating Right to Look Younger
- A Working Mother's Guide to Overcoming the Struggle with the Juggle
- A Working Mother's Guide to a Daily Routine
  and soon to be published, the last in the series
- A Working Mother's Guide to Self-Care

Maggie Webber

Awards and Accolades

Stevie International Business Award

Bronze Award in the 'Best E-book' category, for my Amazon Best-seller titled "A Working Mother's Guide to Blockchain and Cryptocurrency".

Exceptional Women of Excellence

Women Economic Forum awarded the "Exceptional Women of Excellence" award in 2018

Empower KIDs Jury and Global Mentor

Dr. Sarvepalli Radhakrishnan Award by MentorX

I was granted this award today after undertaking a global webinar on "Blockchain and Cryptocurrency - the New Financial Literacy".

Iconic Women Creating a Better World for All

Iconic Women Creating a Better World for All by the Women Economic Forum (WEF) 2019

Contents

Introduction

The 2007 - 2008 Global Financial Crisis brought forth the greatest economic downturn since the Great Depression of 1929. The world's banking systems came crashing down, and unemployment soared while many world governments sought to infuse the economy with a variety of stimulus packages, in order to turn things around.

However, out of this world-changing event, came two things that would revolutionize the world's economy in a more far-reaching manner than any stimulus package.

Blockchain and Cryptocurrency were both new concepts introduced after the world's economy crashed in 2008, and while they were mocked by many at the start of the downturn, they are today being regarded as game-changers that could completely upend the established financial order in the world today.

Cryptocurrency is a totally digital monetary system, the value of which is not based on any individual country's assets or its GDP, and it is only traded as bits and bytes of data on the internet. Blockchain is the information transfer system that cryptocurrencies use for transactions to be undertaken.

These new terms are extremely confusing for anyone not well versed in 'tech. lingo,' but as with the rise of the internet and the ubiquity of smartphones in the last two decades, this is a reality that is going to be imposed on people because of its urgent need in the world today. So much so, people will have no choice but to adapt to this new financial order - or be left behind.

This may sound scary, but it is quite simply the latest in a long line of innovations people have created in order to trade with each other, and to make and save money.

To put things in correct perspective, let us go back in time …

The first people who ever traded material objects did not have any sense of their equivalent value. They simply traded things they wanted, for other things they could give up or do without. However, with the concept of economic need and value, there came the barter system.

This process occurred for many thousands of years, after which the trading of material things like gold, silver, seeds, cloth and spices began. This continued for many centuries, until systems of currency were introduced into regions that were literally backed by gold and silver as the benchmark for their value.

This was succeeded by paper money - first invented in China during the Tang Dynasty, 618 – 907AD. This gave a more uniform look to money, and though it did prove unpopular in the beginning, it eventually caught on and is still being used today to pay for everything from a full tank of gas, to dinner at your local restaurant, or even a house in some parts of the world! (Author's note on 27th October 2020. This may all change of course with Covid-19, whereby the concept of 'dirty money' is now taken very literally and is losing its appeal in many countries.)

Eventually, backing a currency system which used the highest valued precious metal – gold - resulted in the use of the term 'gold standard,' a monetary system in which the standard economic unit of account was based on a fixed quantity of gold, and where a country's currency - fiat or paper money - had its value directly linked to the world price of gold.

Other innovations in the twentieth century have brought forth the use of the checkbook, the greatest benefit of which was that a person could use a check - especially one backed by a bank - to pay huge sums of money that they would feel uncomfortable carrying around in cash. Later, this form of payment was succeeded by credit and debit cards, which can be used to make 'cashless payments' in person, as well as purchases online. Hence, throughout history, the material wealth of nations - and in fact entire regions - has been represented by more and more symbolic objects.

All these monetary innovations bring us to today, where a completely digital currency has not only taken form and proved to be extremely valuable in the eyes of many consumers - but it has also taken the entire world by storm, with its capability to transform the financial landscape of the world into a truly global financial village.

As for Blockchain, the implications of this technology are even more vast than merely cryptocurrency. Since Blockchain is, at its core, a data transfer system which maintains a chain of records – hence the term Blockchain - it can be used to maintain all sorts of records, ranging from healthcare to crop, fishing, music and transport management. Once a process is recorded on Blockchain, any changes made to the information are easy to discover – which results in far more security and transparency of the data that has been stored.

This has vast implications for the world at large, since the digitization of currency, as well as the transformation of entire data transfer systems, can lead to some extremely potent changes. The world can become a more secure place, as a result of cryptographic networks protecting people's privacy. The world can also become free of a lot of 'economic chains', due to cryptocurrencies not being subject to the same restrictions as other national currencies, via banks and governments.

It can also mean there can now be a huge reduction in potential fraud from the misuse of information, if blockchain is the incorruptible vanguard of security that it claims to be.

How is all this possible? Well, that is what this book is here to discuss. The following pages will give you a crash course on what blockchain and cryptocurrencies are and how they work, especially with a focus on the many benefits this will provide to working mothers.

This book also will attempt to chunk this new and often crazy world of financial technology into layperson's terms and bite-sized pieces, and in the process, assist working mothers in understanding some basic concepts, that not even some experts claim to understand fully.

Part 1: What is Blockchain?

Blockchain is the name given to the technology that was invented to transfer the first cryptocurrency, Bitcoin. It is a decentralized ledger made of blocks which contain information about every single transaction made on that Blockchain.

By design, Blockchain resists any modification of data in the blocks that have already been added to the chain. This makes it impenetrable to change, and therefore an extremely secure way in which to store and transfer data.

Blocks

A block is a file that contains information pertinent to that blockchain. It usually contains information about transactions that have occurred on the blockchain but can also contain other information. For instance, the first block ever created on the Bitcoin blockchain included a headline about the UK Chancellor's second bank bailout.

A standard block on the Bitcoin blockchain, when first created, could not exceed 1 MB in size. However, now with the invention of other Blockchains and hard forks on the Bitcoin Blockchain, sizes of blocks have gone up to 128 MB and beyond.

Hash Functions

Hashing is the act of generating a string of values from text using a mathematical function. It is done to encrypt messages by scrambling the text within those messages.

Block Hashes

Block hashes are reference numbers for a block in the blockchain. They are created by cryptographic hash functions.

Cryptographic Hashing

A cryptographic hash function takes any word or message and transforms it into a fixed length number. For Blockchain, a hash function transforms the string into a 256-bit hash. This hash function is called SHA256.

Decentralization

The idea of decentralization is central to blockchain and Bitcoin. Instead of giving control of the technology to a single entity, the inventors of Bitcoin wanted it to be in the hands of as many people as possible. That way, no central entity like banks or governments, could pull the strings and take away the freedom that Bitcoin granted.

This also makes Blockchain a very secure system. Since Blockchain is literally connected through hundreds of thousands of computers which can each monitor and add blocks to the blockchain, this prevents any single entity from changing the record.

All the transactions that have ever been carried out are there for all to see - however the identities of the people who made those transactions are disguised through the hash functions.

The Chain of Digital Signatures

Digital signatures are used to verify or prove identity on blockchain, just as in real life. The difference is that all identities are encrypted on blockchain. While digital signatures are used all over the internet to verify the authenticity of software, games and more, the ones used in blockchain keep changing for each transaction.

Public Key

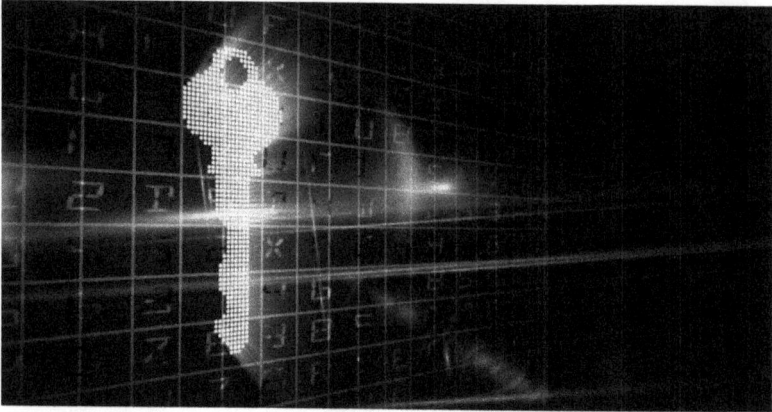

A public signature, also known as a public key, is your public identity on blockchain; it is also known as your Bitcoin wallet address. In some wallets, a new public address is generated every time you make a transaction, so protecting your 'real' one. It is used to verify a transaction when it goes through. It is always generated alongside the private key. Even though they are generated alongside each other, there is no way to determine or derive the private key from the public key.

Private Key

A private key is kept secret with the person who is making the transaction on blockchain. If a message is sent to a person that has been encrypted using their public key, then it is possible for them to decrypt it using their private key. Since the private and public keys are always generated in pairs, it is only possible for a person to decrypt a message that is encrypted with their public key by using their private key.

How a Transaction Occurs

Imagine you want to send some Bitcoin to a friend of yours. The first thing you will need is your friend's bitcoin address, also known as their public key. Then your wallet uses your own private key to generate a new public signature, which can be used to verify the transaction that has occurred.

The public signature is used by nodes on the blockchain network to verify the transaction, and the transaction becomes included in a block along with a few other transactions. Each block includes the hash of the previous block in order to confirm what came before it. This makes sure that the blockchain concerned cannot be tampered with.

Privacy and other Benefits

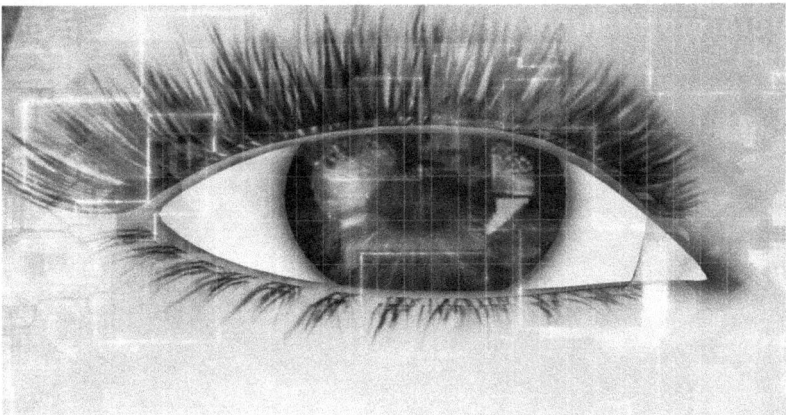

Security

The top benefit of Blockchain is security. There is no other data transfer system on earth that can boast as much data security. Transactions need to be agreed upon before they are approved, and they must be encrypted and linked to previous transactions in order to form a complete chain of data.

Also, since the data is stored across a network of computers, it makes it very hard for hackers to compromise the data in any way.

Speed, Reduced Costs and Efficiency

Market Cap Rank	Cryptocurrency	Average Transaction Speed
1	Bitcoin	78 minutes
2	Ethereum	6 minutes
3	Ripple	4 seconds
4	Bitcoin Cash	60 minutes
5	EOS	1.5 seconds
6	Litecoin	30 minutes
7	Cardano	5 minutes
8	Stellar	5 seconds
9	TRON	5 minutes
10	IOTA	3 minutes
11	NEO	15 seconds
12	Monero	30 minutes
13	Dash	15 minutes
14	NEM	30 seconds
15	VeChain Thor	6 minutes

Source: Coinmarketcap.com

Traditional and paper heavy processes used to transfer money overseas, have generally been perceived to be slow and often creating exorbitant monetary charges. With

23

Blockchain that changes completely. Blockchain uses a single network to transfer data and does not need to convert currency to transfer it from one territory to another.

This reduces the cost and increases the overall efficiency of transferring money. Further, all transactions are approved and documented in a single chain, so there is zero chance of fraud and record tampering.

Also, you can trade in cryptocurrencies from anywhere on the planet. Hence, you do not need to be in one location to trade. Anywhere in the world that allows crypto trading can play a part in the cryptocurrency exchange, as far as you are concerned.

Transparency

The dual advantage of blockchain is it allows complete transparency, without the disadvantage of compromised security. Since blockchain ensures the data of all transactions is stored on a continuous chain, which itself is a decentralized ledger stored on hundreds of thousands of computers, everyone can take a look at all the transactions that have ever occurred.

Financial Independence

Blockchain was built on the foundation of independence and freedom. It really allows anyone and everyone to trade currency, no matter who or where you are in the world. This provides areal and major advantage for women especially, since we usually get the short end of the stick when it comes to wage parity and representation in many of the top professions in the world.

To access a blockchain, all you need is a computer or smartphone and an internet connection, and you are on your way. Further, you do not need huge sums of money, written permission or a 'seat at the table' to get started.

Practical and other Business Uses

Smart Contracts

Smart Contracts are self-executing contracts that can be used to automate the process of entering into agreements. They can ensure the fair and equitable exchange of assets like money, property, shares and more, in such a way that avoids any sort of conflict, and that can eliminate the need for a middleman like a lawyer or an investment banker.

The code that builds a smart contract defines the rules and penalties which surround an agreement such as a traditional contract, but it also allows for certain triggers to be put in place that will automatically execute when certain conditions are fulfilled.

In that instance, if someone faithfully executes the contract, a transfer of assets can take place automatically - and if someone breaks contract, the decided upon penalty can be enforced, without the need for manual action.

Smart contracts can influence large areas in business, especially in healthcare. For example, they can eliminate the need for investigation into healthcare claims, by using objective markers to verify their validity; and can also help in the free exchange of research data among medical research facilities, while keeping the identities of the patient's private via Blockchain.

Smart contracts can also serve as ways to store unalterable records through Blockchain. Since the entire idea of Blockchain depends on records that cannot be altered, smart contracts could act as great digital record keeping software.

DAOs (Decentralized Autonomous Organizations) and DACs (Decentralized Autonomous Corporations)

A DAO is an organization that is decentralized. Instead of a hierarchy which is managed by executives of the company, a specified protocol in the form of Blockchain handles most of the interactions. The blockchain is created so that important contracts can be made, and decisions can be taken objectively, without having to refer to the seniority of a single member of the organization.

DACs are smaller than DAOs and can be sold to the public in the form of shares which are tradeable, but only on the specific blockchain designated. They are subsets of DAOs.

Limitations and Common Misconceptions about Blockchain

- ⬚ Bitcoin is sometimes thought to be an actual physical currency. Many are fooled by images of a gold coin with a 'B' on it, but that is simply the symbol of Bitcoin. There are no actual coins.

- ⬚ You can also buy as little as 1/100 millionth of a Bitcoin, each part being called a 'Satoshi'. You do not have to purchase a whole Bitcoin if you want to invest in this form of cryptocurrency.

- ⬚ Because Bitcoin is completely digital, many believe that it does not have intrinsic value. However, the entire concept of money and worth is the monetary value we place on pieces of paper! We literally just created currencies around the world, and then attached importance to things like gold and copper, simply because we made use of them - when they were both just minerals that we dug up out of the Earth. Similarly, Bitcoin also has intrinsic value, because we have now attached value to it.

28

- Bitcoin is thought to have sunk completely after the boom and bust of 2017, but it has regained more than half its value since that time. And as there is a finite number of Bitcoin - 21 million - that can ever be produced, depending on supply and demand, its value will certainly be reevaluated, and it will not be destroyed or finished soon, if ever.

- Since Bitcoin is known as the first digital currency, people think that it can be shut down like a computer program. This is untrue.

Bitcoin has been used for a lot of illegal and unscrupulous activities - however there is no evidence to suggest that it is used for more illegal deals than hard cash is. The latter is far more untraceable than the former, so criminals still prefer cash to make their deals.

Part 2: Cryptocurrency

The Great Recession

If you are over 15 you may know about something called the Great Recession. Some know it as the 2008 financial crisis or "the biggest economic recession since The Great Depression". There is no doubt that it changed the world and basically birthed the modern 'sharing economy', which is more reliant on technology than ever before. Before 2008 there was no Uber or Airbnb; neither was there a concept of doing individual tasks, getting paid for them and making that your career either, in the way some people do on platforms such as Air-tasker, Upwork or Fiverr.

However, the Great Recession was about much more than that. It was after the 2008 financial crisis that Bitcoin came into existence. Think of it like this. If the system you put all your faith into - literally invested in with all your savings, and trusted it to keep you employed and happy - collapsed, wouldn't you lose faith in that system as well?

Well, that is exactly what happened.

The Great Recession wiped out nearly US$5 trillion from the world economy and rippled throughout the world. Some nations are still struggling with its effects. Hundreds of thousands of jobs and homes were lost, and many people were left without a financial leg to stand on.

Further, it did not help that many governments of the world signed an $850 billion bailout to save the banks, but at the same time left the people to fend for themselves.

Bitcoin was born out of that dissatisfaction with the current system. It was a currency that was free of any control from any bank or a central authority like the government, and instead would be completely decentralized and exchanged through a network which could not be hacked, called blockchain.

It was also completely transparent, since literally thousands of people would be involved in the transactions and so could check if anyone was trying to corrupt this decentralized ledger. Of course, this currency was also not backed by any assets, except for how much faith its buyers and sellers had in it – and this is rather like the faith we put in fiat currencies as well, of course.

However, the idea of being free of the corrupt system that had caused the Great Recession was just too sweet to pass up. And so, the idea of cryptocurrency was born, and like a genie that has been let out of a bottle, it could never be put back in.

What is a Cryptocurrency?

If you have ever wondered what a cryptocurrency is, you are not alone. Most people who aren't enthusiasts, or people who do not keep up with the news, or even those who have read up something about Bitcoin and Ethereum, will not be able to tell you what cryptocurrency is.

In layperson's terms, a Cryptocurrency is digital currency that uses cryptography for security. Cryptocurrency is completely digital and is not based on any currency that exists in the real world, nor any asset owned by a country, a bank or a private organization; there are exceptions to these rules of course, but none of the major cryptocurrencies like Bitcoin or Ethereum are backed by real assets.

This is completely new territory for currency, and therefore Bitcoin was mocked in its initial days as doomed to fail.

Another big feature of cryptocurrencies is that they allow for secure payments. These payments are far more secure than the ones that are made through any banking system or government mandated financial system in the world. This is because the transfer system that cryptocurrencies use is immutable and transparent – and it is called blockchain.

Cryptocurrencies use cryptography and lots of encryption algorithms in order to secure their transactions. And blockchain ensures the transfers are recorded into a decentralized ledger.

What this means is, any transaction that happens on a single blockchain will be recorded by every single node in the network. This way, there will be no way to change the ledger or corrupt the data, without everyone else on the network noticing – and this is because everyone on the network has access to a copy of that ledger.

The third and final major element of a cryptocurrency is that it can be transferred anywhere in the world through the internet, without any middlemen fees being incurred. This has been a major bone of contention for consumers with previous systems of money transfer. If they must send money from one bank to the next, to another city or even another country, then they need to deal with an increasing scale of fees. Cryptocurrencies simply offer fixed, minimal processing fees that do not change, no matter where you want to send money.

Hence, a currency that allows you to break free of a financial system - which is viewed by many as corrupt, allows you to be secure in the knowledge that your transactions are monitored and essentially un-hackable, and allows you to bypass the fees imposed by banks and governments, is bound to generate interest. And that is exactly why Bitcoin has become so popular, so quickly.

Who invented Bitcoin and Blockchain?

If you want the short answer, it is that no one really knows. No one has been able to unmask or interview the individual – or possibly the group of people - who came up with the concept of Bitcoin. But if you want the answer that everyone gives when asked that question, it is 'Satoshi Nakamoto'.

Satoshi Nakamoto

Satoshi Nakamoto is the pseudonym given to the individual or group responsible for birthing Bitcoin and Blockchain. No one has been able to unmask who this person or group is, though there are certainly many guesses as to who it may be, and candidates for the identity of Nakamoto usually come from a computer science and/or cryptography background.

Satoshi Nakamoto is said to reside or have been born in Japan. In October of 2008, they published a paper called, "Bitcoin: A Peer-to-Peer Electronic Cash System". The document was signed Satoshi Nakamoto, right below the title of the document. Following this, the first Bitcoin software was introduced in January of 2009 and the Bitcoin network came into existence. The first Block of Bitcoin – called the 'Genesis' or 'Zero' block - was created, and within that first block of data was embedded in the text, "The Times 03/Jan/2009 Chancellor on brink of second bailout for banks". This eliminates any doubt that Bitcoin was created as a response to the dissatisfaction with the banking system at large, and the handling of the Great Recession by governments around the world.

Subsequent updates followed, and more information began to flow out about how Bitcoin would work, and how it was to be developed. As to the identity of Nakamoto, nothing was known. Finally, after years of working on the currency, he/she/they handed the control of development over to Gavin Andresen - a software developer - who himself resigned that role in 2012.

Candidates for who Nakamoto could be, include the following:

Nick Szabo

He was one of the first people suspected of being Satoshi Nakamoto. Since he published a paper called 'Bit Gold', which was a precursor to cryptocurrency, he was a natural candidate.

A reverse analysis of the text in the paper revealed that it had several similarities to the Bitcoin paper published by Satoshi Nakamoto in October of 2008. Combined with the fact that a lot of Bit Gold's ideas have been used by Bitcoin, but never referenced directly, all this evidence makes him a prime candidate for inventing Bitcoin. However, he denies any involvement.

Dorian Prentice Satoshi Nakamoto

Yes. there is an actual Japanese/American working in science today, who is named Satoshi Nakamoto. However, this person is a physicist at California Polytechnic University.

He is also a self-proclaimed libertarian, and therefore would subscribe to the philosophy behind Bitcoin.

He has been suspected to be the founder of Bitcoin for a while now, and even once made the statement that he was no longer involved 'in it' and 'I cannot discuss it'. This led people to believe that he was the legendary founder after all. However, he recanted on that position in a later interview, citing he thought the question was related to his classified work as a military contractor.

David Kleiman

He was involved in the beginnings of Bitcoin, since he was one of the earliest miners. He has also designed systems used by the highest levels of the US government to secure its digital systems, so he is a pretty good candidate.

He unfortunately became a paraplegic in a motorcycle accident and died in 2013.

Hal Finney

Hal Finney was ostensibly the first person ever to receive Bitcoin when Satoshi Nakamoto sent him 10 Bitcoins as a test. He also corresponded with Nick Szabo and lived a few blocks away from Dorian Prentice Satoshi Nakamoto.

His involvement in filing bug reports, making use of the original bitcoin software and suggesting improvements to the overall program, are all cited as evidence of him being the founder of Bitcoin.

However, this is all circumstantial at best. Unfortunately for the world, if he were Satoshi Nakamoto, we will never get to hear it from him, as he too passed away - in August of 2014.

Bitcoin

Bitcoin is the first cryptocurrency, and it was created in 2009. It is the most popular cryptocurrency in the world and has achieved the greatest success in the digital currency world out of all the currencies on the market right now. It is regarded by many as 'the Mother Ship', and what Bitcoin does on the market, all other alt. coins tend to follow.

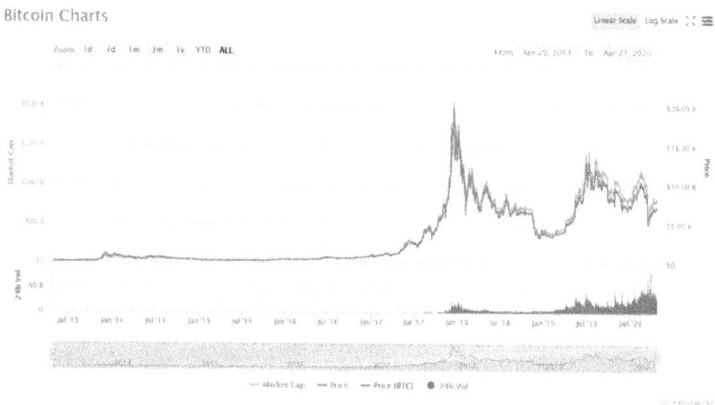

Source: Coinmarketcap.com

In 2017, the currency hit an all-time high value of US$20,000, before the bubble burst and the currency started to lose value. It has begun to gain value again as of early 2019, with its market value reaching nearly $9,000 in June 2019.

Bitcoin has attracted both the praise and the ire of many individuals, corporations and government agencies around the world. People have called it the greatest step forward for money in the history of the world, while others have called it an instrument of crime.

The latter is a charge leveled against it because of the illegal trading that goes on through Bitcoin, and the number of illegal assets seized every single year by governments around the world. It has also been banned by several governments including China, India, and Pakistan, though many of these governments have softened their stance on Cryptocurrency of late.

Bitcoin has been recognized as a genuine challenger to the world's set economic order, as more and more people are becoming enthusiastic about the difference it could make.

How does Bitcoin work?

You can begin investing in and trading with Bitcoin, without knowing many of the details behind how it works, if you just want to conduct transactions. It is very simple to install a Bitcoin wallet on your phone or your computer. Once you have done that, the wallet will generate a Bitcoin address for you. Think of this like an IP address for your internet connection, but this will be specific to your Bitcoin wallet. Just as an IP address is used to send data to a source, your Bitcoin address will be used to send cryptocurrency to your wallet.

The address will be 34 characters long and is also known as a public key. This will be visible to everyone who wants to send you funds and who is conducting transactions with you.

However, the Bitcoin address or public key also corresponds to a private key which is 64 characters long. This is private to you and only you can see it.

The reason for this is that public keys can change from transaction to transaction, but private keys remain the same. Private keys can be used to log into your wallet and sign off on the transaction conducted, when combined with the public key.

The keys are related - but there is no way to determine one if you have the other.

Transactions

Using the two keys, the Bitcoin wallet can generate a digital signature which is sent to the Blockchain network for validation. For a Bitcoin transaction to go through, 51% of the nodes within the network need to validate the transaction.

The transaction is validated with a combination of the public key and the digital signature generated from the combination of the public and private keys. Hence, no one else ever sees the private key.

Once the transaction has been validated, it becomes added to the blockchain as part of and in the form of a block.

Every single transaction on the Bitcoin blockchain is recorded, and is ordered sequentially, depending on when it is validated.

Mining

BITCOIN MINING

You may have heard of Bitcoin mining before, but you may not know what the term means. In layperson's terms, it is the use of computer processing power to solve complex mathematical problems, in order to create Bitcoin.

Hence, if you continue the mining metaphor, the computer is the pickaxe, and the Bitcoin is the gold. However, as you can imagine, the deeper you drill into the mine, the harder it becomes to find gold, and eventually the mine runs dry. The same is the case with Bitcoin.

The more Bitcoin is generated, the harder it gets to mine for more. In fact, the founders of Bitcoin created the software in such a manner, that when a limit of 21 million Bitcoins is reached, no new Bitcoins can be generated (or it will get so hard to generate Bitcoins that it will be pointless to even try). This limit is currently estimated to be reached sometime in 2140. Currently (November 2019) there are more than 17.7 million Bitcoins in circulation.

Why is this? To find that out, we need to take a closer look in to the mining process.

Confirming Transactions

The only way to mine Bitcoin is by confirming transactions. All the computers confirming and validating transactions on the Bitcoin blockchain, are doing so by solving complex algorithms on their computers.

To do this, they are using up huge amounts of processing power — and the larger the amount of a transaction, the more confirmations are needed. Hence, if a payment is less than US$1000, there is a need for only one confirmation. Two confirmations are needed for payments from US$1000 to US$10,000. And three confirmations are needed for payments between US$10,000 and US$1,000,000.

Now you may be wondering, what do these complex algorithms want to find that requires so much computing power? It is an integer that lies between 0 and

4,294,967,296. This number is not just randomly selected; it is combined with the data in the block and pushed through the hash function in order to confirm the transaction.

This number is called a 'nonce' – a term that means a 'number that can only be used once'.

This is harder than it sounds and takes more and more computing power in order to get right, every single second that passes. As mentioned before, the program is designed so there can only ever be a total of 21 million Bitcoins at any point in time. At this moment, 84.61% of that limit of Bitcoins have been mined, and the total number of Bitcoins which are left to mine is just over 3.2 million.

Block Reward

A Block Reward refers to the new Bitcoins that are mined and awarded to the Bitcoin miner who has confirmed a certain transaction and added a block to the chain. Every single block is around 1 MB in size.

In the beginning of Bitcoin, every single block reward was 50 Bitcoins. But since the 21 million Bitcoin limit was enforced from the beginning, the Bitcoin block reward is halved every single time 210,000 Blocks are added to the chain. Hence, after 64 iterations of the reward being halved, the value of a block reward will become near zero.

At this time (December 2019) the block reward is 12.5 Bitcoins, and from the 21st of May 2020, it to be halved to 6.25 Bitcoins.

Transaction Time

The average time for a Bitcoin block transaction is 10 minutes. However, it takes far longer for a transaction to be validated. Before a transaction is validated, it goes into a pool of unconfirmed transactions called the Bitcoin mempool. There Bitcoin miners can pick up these transactions. Hence, the ten-minute waiting period.

However, the Bitcoin transaction validation process can sometimes even take days. The reason for that can be congestion on the Blockchain, or the fees that are attached to the Bitcoin transaction.

Also, since miners love to get paid - and who doesn't, they tend to take transactions that have the highest fees attached to them or those are the largest transactions. So, if you are sending out a dollar to somebody in Bitcoin, get ready to wait - because there maybe someone sending a thousand dollars at the same time, and they will be first in the queue.

Taxes & Fees

Can you be taxed on the crypto assets you hold or on the transactions that you engage in? The short answer is yes, though it is complicated.

While originally Bitcoin and Blockchain were non-taxable, since they were a blip on the radar of world governments and central banks, today that is not the case. So, let us first deal with the fees that are associated with cryptocurrency transactions.

Transaction Fees

Every transaction that is made on the Bitcoin blockchain must be validated by miners on the blockchain network. If you attach a fee with that transaction, that is more incentive for the miner to validate that transaction. That way, the higher you pay, the more likely your transaction is to go through faster.

The minimum fee that you can pay for a transaction to go through the blockchain varies, and it depends on how crowded the network is at the time. If you pay a higher fee, more miners will try to get that transaction verified faster, since everyone likes to get paid.

However, even with this incentivized system, there is still the freedom for Bitcoin to be transferred around the world, without incurring any of the extra fees that are commonly charged for foreign exchange.

Then there is the belief that Bitcoin cannot be taxed. That was the case - but now Bitcoin taxes have been introduced in many countries around the world that have come to recognize the value of cryptocurrency. Even in Malta - the European country that has branded itself as 'Blockchain Island', and which has passed a series of laws that have encouraged the trade of Bitcoin in the nation - crypto transactions are taxed.

Various finance regulators around the world, such as the IRS in the US, have made it their mission to target people who are hiding crypto assets. I totally agree this should be the case

- and the quicker the better, as this will help global acceptance of this form of currency and people trading with it. Just as with everything else you earn and own, you need to pay taxes on crypto assets, so you do not get in trouble with the law.

Be sure to look up the law regarding cryptocurrency in your state as well as in your country and find out if you are liable to pay taxes on the Bitcoin you mined back in 2010.

Ethereum

Ethereum is the second largest cryptocurrency in the world by market capitalization. It is operated by a Swiss non-profit called the Ethereum Foundation. The Ethereum network offers a lot of potential uses to customers, who can use it for far more than conducting simple transactions. They can use it to enhance the functionality of their Blockchain technology and speed up processes, operations and workflows.

Ethereum is fundamentally different from Bitcoin, in that it does not want to disrupt the financial world, as much as it wants to change the way data is transferred over the internet. Ethereum's implementation would impact third parties who store data, transfer mortgages and keep track of financial instruments.

The World Computer

Ethereum wants to be a 'World Computer', one that would decentralize the current client-server model the internet operates on. This would essentially democratize the internet model to a degree not imagined before.

Imagine all the servers and clouds responsible for storing and beaming out data to the world were replaced by nodes. These nodes would be hundreds of thousands—and eventually millions—of people who would be sitting at their computers, serving as connections or links on a huge global chain; hence the term 'World Computer.'

If you follow the HBO comedy show "Silicon Valley", you would probably have heard of something like this being espoused by the lead character, Richard Hendricks.

Ethereum's vision is to enable the same type of functionality to every single person across the world, so everyone could compete to offer services that overlay this infrastructure, if they so choose. This could be in the form of apps or additional hardware that could run on a smartphone.

With that said, the Decentralized Apps system would be different from the current app stores we know of (such as Apple App Store and Google Play Store), which depend on storing your personal information on an email account in order to complete a transaction and require your credit card information for apps that are not free of charge.

Hence, the information you provide to them is controlled by third parties, and you cannot purchase anything without a third-party confirmation. The choice of apps is also governed by the handlers of the app store, and not the makers of the app themselves. Only the apps that pass strict standards end up on these platforms. While this is a good thing for security, it does leave out a lot of app creators and software programmers, who are often not able to get their apps through the stringent process required by the store reps., even though they may not have any major bugs or security issues. Also, these app stores take a massive 30% cut of the profits, which could well go back into to go the creator's future Research and Development.

Ethereum would allow the person making the app to retain control of data with these services. Hence, if you are the creator of the app, the E book or the service you want to sell, then all the profits will go to you, and you will be the deciding factor in whether your app makes it into people's smartphones and computers, rather than the platform itself.

The 'World Computer' will ensure that no one entity will have control over the infrastructure responsible for delivering products and services and, most importantly, knowledge to you. No one could suddenly ban a service they deem horrible or offensive or not strictly in line with their personal guidelines. And while this may cause dismay with some people, it is also a very freeing development in a world that has become so censored and restricted.

The idea has been met with great skepticism, as is the case with most technologies, and it is not certain yet which blockchain apps will prove fruitful or end up on the Ethereum blockchain - and there is also no proof as to how scalable, how secure and how useful those apps will be. All these questions will only be answered with time.

Other top Alt. Coins

Ever since the invention of Bitcoin, other cryptocurrencies have materialized and have begun competing with the original. While some have come from independent coders and others are backed by major corporations, all of them are trying to take advantage of the craze of cryptocurrencies, in order to turn a profit.

Ripple (XRP)

Ripple was founded as a payment-transfer system in 2005, by a company called Open-Coin. It was rebranded as Ripple Labs in 2015. The goal of Ripple is to make a payments system that can act as a universal currency exchange over the internet. The actual currency is called Ripple, and the network over which it is exchanged is called Ripple-Net.

In order to make sure its range is extended globally, Ripple Labs has made deals with various financial institutions around the world, including ones in India, Australia, and, most recently, Latin America. It is currently the third largest cryptocurrency in the world by market capitalization.

Litecoin

Litecoin is the fourth largest cryptocurrency in the world and is based on open-source cryptographic protocols. It is not managed by any company or central authority. When we talk about the technicalities of the currency, it is quite similar to Bitcoin as it was originally a spinoff to it when it was born in 2011.

The key difference between Bitcoin and Litecoin is that Litecoin claims to be much faster and processes a block every 2.5 minutes, instead of the 10 minutes that Bitcoin takes. Also, the developers of Litecoin claim that it is much faster in confirming transactions than Bitcoin.

Bitcoin Cash

Bitcoin Cash was a hard fork from the original Bitcoin and came into existence when a group of developers wanted to increase the block size limit of Bitcoin. The hard fork took effect in August 2017 and, as a result, the Bitcoin ledger split into two – therefore Bitcoin Cash was born.

As a result, Bitcoin Cash allows larger blocks on the blockchain, and this allows it to process far more transactions per second than Bitcoin. However, then Bitcoin Cash split into two cryptocurrencies as well in November of 2018, and that second cryptocurrency became Bitcoin SV.

Bitcoin SV (Bitcoin Satoshi's Vision)

Bitcoin SV or Bitcoin Satoshi's Vision is a branch-off of Bitcoin Cash which claims to restore Bitcoin to Satoshi Nakamoto's vision. As outlined previously, Satoshi Nakamoto is the original founder - or a member of the original group of founders - of Bitcoin.

The split occurred in Bitcoin Cash between two rival factions; one was called Bitcoin ABC, while the other was called Bitcoin SV. The arguments between the two were over Block sizes. The former wanted Block sizes to remain at 32 MB while the latter, BSV, had promoted a code that would increase the block size limit to 128 MB.

USDT (Tether)

Tether is a controversial cryptocurrency that was issued by Tether limited. Each token was claimed to be backed by $1. However, in March of 2019, the Attorney General of the State of New York accused Bitfinex, the crypto exchange the currency was being traded on, of covering up nearly $850 million in funds that had been missing since 2018.

Another investigation into Tether concerns the 'Bitcoin Boom and Bust of 2017'. Tether has been accused by Professor John M. Griffin and his student Amin Shams, both of whom are from the University of Texas, of price manipulation of Bitcoin in 2017.

According to their research published in a paper titled "Is Bitcoin Really Untethered?", half the price increases in Bitcoin could be traced back to the trading of Tether that occurred on the Bitfinex exchange in 2017.

Calibra

Calibra is the name of the wallet that Facebook has created, in order to produce its own cryptocurrency called Libra. The currency, which is said to be launching in 2020, will have a larger reach than any that is currently in circulation, due to the unequalled reach Facebook has all over the planet.

Facebook's 2.7 billion active monthly users will have access to Libra to exchange through smartphone apps, web apps and Facebook's other apps like WhatsApp, Instagram and Messenger. The move has generated a new wave of interest in digital currencies, and the question of whether this will allow Facebook to achieve an unwarranted level of control over more than a third of the world's population is something currently before the US Congress.

A token is nothing more than an 'unique string' - and we use tokens and certs every day on the web, every time we go to a https website - so this is now the norm for most of us.

Crypto Tokens are tradable assets or utilities, that are somewhat like cryptocurrency, in that they can be traded and exchanged the same way - but they are different insofar as they can only be exchanged and traded for specific things.

Crypto Tokens are special virtual currency tokens which reside on special blockchains that can represent an asset or utility. For example, a crypto token can represent customer loyalty points that can be exchanged for discounts; or there can be crypto tokens which can be exchanged for a prize being given out by an organization. We are even seeing football clubs like the Spanish team 'Barcelona' being tokenized!

Crypto tokens can serve as transaction units on blockchains which are created using the standard templates like the Ethereum network, which also allows the freedom to create as many tokens as you like.

These blockchains work on the premise of decentralized apps or smart contracts, so they do not need any sort of independent verification. Instead, they rely on automatic triggers which can verify transactions, and exchange the tokens for their equivalent upon receiving them.

These tokens are often distributed through something called an Initial Coin Offering (ICO).

How do Coins, Stablecoins, and Tokens differ?

Cryptocurrencies are also known as **coins** in the digital world. There are many on the market such as Bitcoin, Ethereum, Litecoin, and 2000 + more. Their value can rise and fall depending on the trading that goes on in their Blockchains - and they are known to be quite volatile in certain cases, as there is nothing backing them, like the assets of a country or GDP per capita, or the reserves of a bank.

Stablecoins however, are cryptocurrencies that are deliberately designed so their value deviation is minimized, and hence their volatility in the market is minimized as well.

A stablecoin can be attached to a currency, or to exchange any such traded commodities like gold, silver or other precious metals.

Stablecoins are redeemable in commodities, and they are said to be backed by actual assets - hence they are considered more trustworthy than some other cryptocurrencies.

Tokens are not attached to currencies and can only be exchanged for specific things. They cannot be used in order to exchange different types of currencies, and they cannot be used in order to trade in all types of tradable commodities. They are assigned for one purpose and can only be used for that purpose.

Initial Coin Offering (ICO)

Blockchain equity funding pales in comparison to ICOs
Quarterly blockchain equity and ICO financing. Q3'16 - Q4'17

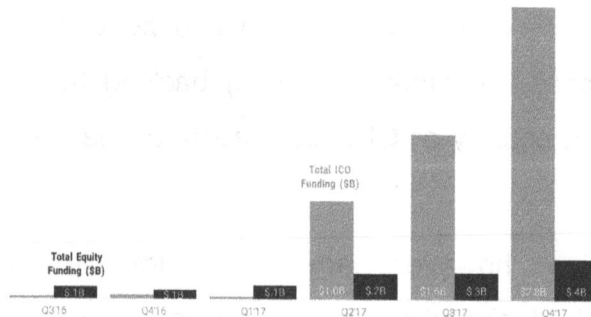

Total Equity Funding ($B)						
Total ICO Funding ($B)						

Source: CB Insights, TokenData

CBINSIGHTS

Source: CBS Insights

If you are not familiar with stock market trading and the terms used, you may have a little trouble understanding what an ICO is - so I will chunk things down a little.

Imagine you run a successful company. That company will need financial backing it if it is to grow. The money will come from investors, and in return for that money, they will want part ownership of your company. So, in exchange for the money they invest, you will give them shares which can be thought of as small parts in the ownership of your company.

Now, let us say you want to expand your company beyond the amount your investors can fund - so you write a prospectus, take your company public, and you allow the public to purchase shares from your company. Your company needs to be listed on a stock exchange for the public to do this. If all goes well, the company's shares are bought for market price, and its value shoots through the roof. This is called an Initial Public Offering or an IPO.

Now an Initial Coin Offering or an ICO is somewhat similar, except it is for cryptocurrencies and crypto related systems only. It involves putting your idea up online; having a White Paper published; a RoadMap designed, which outlines the steps intended and the dates these steps will occur by; and asking people to give you money in exchange for tokens or cryptocurrency, so you can fund your new project.

The tokens the public purchase can act like shares in a company, and if the currency increases in circulation, then your investors can gain from their initial investment.

To make a few things very clear, buying the ICO will not actually give you ownership in a company, and you are essentially gambling with your wealth, as the idea put online has nothing backing it, except the word of someone you have never laid eyes on, or even talked to in most cases.

What is more concerning, is that anyone can launch an ICO and without any regulation. Unlike IPOs, which must be under regulation by the various financial laws and regulations in whatever country they occur, ICOs do not have to answer to anyone. Therefore, there have been many examples of ICOs which turned out to be fraudulent - so-called 'pump-and-dump' schemes–that are without any value.

Hence, an ICO is like an IPO in name only, and that is why they are now seen by many as a scam, and sadly are a fraud in many cases.

STO (Security Token Offering)

An STO or Security Token Offering, is like an Initial Coin Offering, but before you recoil in horror, please know that it is actually very different to an ICO in one major respect; it is secure. Instead of giving out unknown bits of cryptocurrency to you in exchange for your fiat currency, Ethereum or Bitcoin, an STO will give out a Security Token.

This is comparable to an investment contract between the two of you. The security token will represent an asset, like stocks, bonds and funds. This makes it much safer than an ICO, and much more like an IPO.

In an IPO, your investment is listed down through a digital certificate, and saved so that it is listed in your name. The same thing is done with an STO, except that the information is listed on a Blockchain. It is this overlap with an IPO, that makes the STO such a secure investment, especially when compared to an ICO.

STO v IPO

Both being regulated offerings, the differences between an STO and IPO are comparable to the differences between paper money and coins. They are both separated by time, and one is more convenient than the other.

STOs are said to be more cost-effective than IPOs, the main reason being that going to the market with an IPO involves brokerage and investment banking fees, as well often very high legal fees. STOs are an alternative requiring much less financial and time investment, on the part of the seller and the purchaser. They offer more direct access to the investment market, so there are not as many large fees involved, and the post offering administration is also much less of a challenge too.

Because of all these reasons STOs are a more inexpensive option. Also due to the removal of middlemen - like bankers, brokerage agents and other professionals, who often have had an air of mistrust around them, especially since the GFC in 2008 - the change for the investment market has been welcomed by many.

There is also the ease of being able to trade 24/7, that comes with an STO. Since the stock market is limited to the trading day for only five days a week, the STO provides an infinite window of trading - and this also brings more liquidity to the markets that the security tokens represent, including assets like property, collectibles and even expensive art.

Further, STOs open trading to a much larger section of the market, who normally would not have access - people like you and me, and the average Jane and Joe, even people in remote areas, who do not have access to a bank or even a bank account. And because STOs are compliant with the authorities, they present far less risk for an investor – another good reason to encourage more investors to come on board.

STO Bans

Even though STOs are much more reliable than ICOs, they have been banned by many countries, due to the mistrust surrounding Bitcoin and cryptocurrencies in general. There is also the matter of cryptocurrencies not answering to the tax laws of a country, which seems to get under the skin of a lot of governments and banks. Ironically, some of these same countries are now talking about creating their own cryptocurrency, which seems to fly in the face of why they want crypto banned in the first place.

Nevertheless, the countries that have banned STOs include China, South Korea, Vietnam, Algeria, Morocco, Namibia, Zimbabwe, Bolivia, India, Lebanon, Nepal, Bangladesh, and Pakistan.

Why is a STO better than an ICO?

Compared to an ICO, STO's are much more reliable and lower risk. Since there are authorities that regulate STOs, investors like you and me feel far more trusting about the money we invest. And of course, it is natural that more transparency encourages far greater trust.

Tips to Invest Smartly in Cryptocurrencies

If you are a new cryptocurrency investor, then you will need some training and education before you find the best coins to invest in. Here are a few tips to help you invest in the crypto game, even if you are a novice:

Getting Started with Cryptocurrency Investing

- The first thing that you need to know is that cryptocurrency is not a fad or a simple trend that will go away. No matter what the naysayers shout from their ivory towers, cryptocurrency represents a shift in global finance and economics.

- The second thing that you need to know is that cryptocurrency is new and volatile. As evidenced by the 2017 'Bitcoin boom and bust', cryptocurrency has not found its bearings yet. It will probably take at least a decade or so for it to become normalized for free trade, plus the endorsement of various banks and governments, for it to become more and truly stable.

- Hence, you should always perform your due diligence before you invest in any cryptocurrency. Whether it's Bitcoin, Ripple, Ether or Litecoin, there needs to be concrete logic behind your investment decisions. 'Sentiment' and 'good feelings' about a certain share do not cut it on Wall Street, so they should not here either.

- Also, please do not get into any 'pump and dump strategies' which only seek to make money quickly, and then get out of the cryptocurrency just as fast. These schemes have been used many a time to fool investors and to make quick bucks for the founders. They are equivalent to a modern-day snake oil salesman. 'Smoke and Mirrors', and a lot of hot air.

- Another important tip is diversification. Just as your portfolio should include investments into a variety of stocks, so that your overall profits and losses are not dependent on a single stock, so should your crypto assets be diverse, so that the collapse of a single coin does not wipe out your liquidity.

▫ Be wary of mobile wallets. Right now, there are a few mobile wallets on the market that purport to be extremely secure and built for storing crypto assets. However, that is simply too much of a risk to take. Though it is convenient to carry around your crypto assets in your pocket, these can be burgled very easily, and hence should not be an option you consider. Maybe just a few dollars in hot storage, for ease of access if you want to invest – otherwise it is cold storage and a 2FA authentication process all the way.

The World's Best Crypto-Exchanges

Like stock exchanges, there are cryptocurrency exchanges around the world that you can rely onto trade in all manner of cryptocurrencies, and all under one roof. The fees differ hugely and there are thousands of crypto exchanges out there today, but these are the most reliable:

Coinbase

One of the first crypto exchanges to be launched, Coinbase is based in San Francisco and allows users to withdraw and deposit funds quite easily. It offers advanced security and a user-friendly interface. But the fees are quite high, unless you use Coinbase Pro.

Binance

This is one of the biggest crypto exchanges in the world today and supports trading with 130 cryptocurrencies. This includes Bitcoin, Ripple, Bitcoin Cash, Ethereum and GAS. Binance offers standard fees of about 0.1%.

BitMex

BitMex supports Ethereum, Litecoin, Ripple, Cardano and Bitcoin Cash, as well as other cryptocurrencies apart from Bitcoin. The fee structure is very straightforward and inexpensive.

Bittrex

Based in the US, Bittrex allows you to trade with 190 crypto currencies, and is regulated under US crypto laws. The standard service fee is 0.25% and only requires you to register via email.

KuCoin

This crypto exchange offers a fully functional mobile app for both iOS and Android. You can trade several different cryptocurrencies at this crypto-exchange, and its fees are dependent on the currency you trade in and withdrawals that you make.

Huobi

Founded in China, it supports about 250 cryptocurrencies. You can use the crypto exchange to trade fiat currencies for crypto assets at zero fees, or you can even upgrade to Huobi Pro, which is designed for advanced trading capabilities and has a fee structure of 0.2%.

Kraken

This crypto exchange offers many fiat currencies as well as 17 cryptocurrencies. You can trade in the US Dollar, the Pound and the Yen, as well as in Bitcoin, Ethereum, Tether and more. The fees range from 0% to 0.26%.

Trading Cryptocurrencies in a Legal and Regulated Market

Depending on where you live, there are several different bodies and laws governing cryptocurrency exchange and trade around the world. In some major countries, the trade and purchase of cryptocurrencies is completely banned, while in places like Malta, it is incentivized and encouraged.

Look up the laws in your Country and your State/Province relating to cryptocurrencies, before you make any decisions at all.

Storing Cryptocurrency safely with Bitcoin Wallets

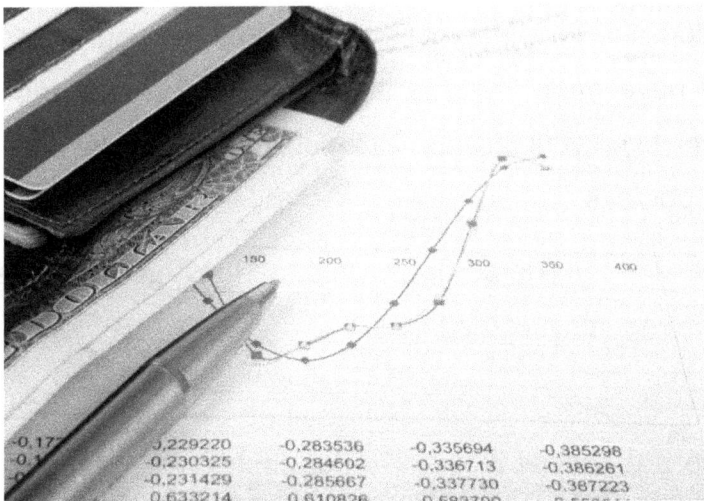

In order to store Bitcoin or any other form of cryptocurrency you need to have a wallet. These not only hold your address from which you can transfer and to which you can send Bitcoin, but they also keep your crypto assets secure.

Hardware Wallets

These can come in the form of hard drives and flash drives. Specialized hardware wallets are optimized for crypto storage. They are the best option from a security point of view. Since they are disconnected from the internet most of the time, they are called cold wallets. Even though they are expensive, they are well worth the investment.

Desktop Wallets

This basically means installing wallet software on your desktop and keeping your crypto assets on your computer. They have more features than other wallets and allow full control over your assets with public and private keys and seed phrases.

These are considered hot wallets, as they are connected to the internet most of the time.

Mobile Wallets

These are special mobile phones that have been designed for security and to function as Bitcoin storage devices. A few of these have been promoted on the market for businessmen and investors, such as the Sikur Phone. However, they are expensive, and as they are vulnerable to theft, it may not be wise to choose this option.

Wallets

All wallets are online wallets at some stage in the process, even cold wallets (unless they are paper ones) and this means they are the least secure option for storing crypto assets. The only advantage is that you have constant accessibility. You can open this wallet on every single device you own and can access it from any point on earth. However, that open access is exactly what makes the process and your investments so insecure.

Paper Wallets

This is the most secure wallet since you cannot hack into paper. 'Paper wallet' is a general term for a wallet of any type, the login details and keys of which are written down on physical paper.

You can, of course, lose this paper anywhere if you are not careful, and this can make your Bitcoin stash vulnerable to theft. However, it all depends on how responsible you are with your critical information.

Securing your Financial Future through Blockchain and Cryptocurrency

Investing in Bitcoin and other cryptocurrencies can feel scary. But it really is not as complicated as most people think.

Just like any other investment, you should only invest a portion of your income into cryptocurrency. Use Mark Cuban's advice, which is to invest 10% of your savings into Bitcoin, Ether, Ripple, Litecoin, Bitcoin Cash, and so on. This makes sure that you have enough of your savings stable in a bank account, and enough invested so your investments can grow.

Do your research on which currencies are the safest to invest in. Usually, this advice can be found online on forums like Bitcoin talk. Also, invest in the Blue-chip cryptocurrencies, which have a total market capitalization of over $2 billion.

Keep checking on the value of cryptocurrencies every day and a great website to do this is coinmarketcap.com

Keep up with the news on the cryptocurrency that you have invested in, buy low and sell high, just as in the stock market game.

Never accept 'good sentiment' or 'rising value' or 'great potential' as a good reason to invest in a cryptocurrency, without looking at the underlying reasons they are described as this first. I also check very carefully into the backgrounds of the management team behind a project, and whether their project is sustainable and one that will truly assist the planet and be in demand.

Keep your ear to the ground for the latest cryptocurrencies and learn as much about each one before you decide to invest. Bitcointalk.org is a great place to start.

Finally, remember that cryptocurrencies are not a fad. They are the next step in the evolution of money. This is what money and global finance will become soon, no matter how much anyone denies it– so why not become an early adopter, and make strong some gains with your investments before everyone else realizes the many benefits of this exciting and quickly growing marketplace?

Final Note

Cryptocurrency and blockchain are both instruments that are disrupting the current economic system. They were created to not only do that, but to give the world an increased level of economic freedom. These tools weren't created for the celebrity living in a mansion in Beverly Hills, but for the single mother dropping her kids to school, or the entrepreneur coming up with the next Microsoft.

The 21st Century has brought various engines of change into our homes. They range from computers in our pockets, to 24-hour global connectivity, to data as currency. And that last part is the most important.

Know that Blockchain and Bitcoin aren't words to be feared, but to be embraced. They are systems that were built for us to leave behind the chains of economic oppression, that the big banks and big governments had thrown around our necks and ankles. Know that these are the tools you can use, to not only invest in and build your life with, but also to irrevocably change it.

This book should not be the end of your journey, but a stepping off point into the vast world of Cryptocurrency. Try investing in some Ethereum, go learn about blockchain programming or about the different Crypto exchanges in your country.

So…Go explore. Go build. Go Crypto.

If you want to learn more about building the right mindset to secure an abundant future using Cryptocurrency, you may like to take one of Maggie's courses or do some coaching with her.

Please go to www.maggiewebber.com or send her an email on contact@maggiewebber.com

She looks forward to hearing from you soon.

www.ingramcontent.com/pod-product-compliance
Lightning Source LLC
Chambersburg PA
CBHW070945210326
41520CB00021B/7064